G000296904

The Significance of A Dress

Emma Lee

ARACHNE PRESS

First published in UK 2020 by Arachne Press Limited
100 Grierson Road, London SE23 1NX
www.arachnepress.com
© Emma Lee 2020
ISBN: 978-1-909208-83-4

The moral rights of the author has been asserted.
All content is copyright the author.
All rights reserved. This book is sold subject to the condition that it shall not by way of trade or otherwise, be lent, resold, hired out or otherwise circulated without the publisher's prior written consent in any form or binding or cover other than that in which it is published and without similar condition including this condition being imposed on the subsequent purchaser.
Except for short passages for review purposes no part of this publication may be reproduced, stored in a retrieval system or transmitted in any form, or by any means, electronic, mechanical, photocopying, recording or otherwise without prior written permission of Arachne Press Limited.
Thanks to Muireann Grealy for her proofing.
Printed on wood-free paper in the UK by TJ International, Padstow.

First Publication Acknowledgements

A Boy's Text Message in Headlines in Picaroon Poetry 2016

An Elephant in Atlantic City, Gone Midnight and I Needed to Press Reset, He Did/She Did, Today's Lesson Misses the Target, Uniforms Contain People, and *Where No One Operates the Lights,* in Winedrunk Sidewalk Adventures in Trumpland (USA) 2018 and 2019

Bridal Dresses in Beirut in Dreamcatcher 2019 and in The Red Earth Review (USA) 2019

Diary from Holloway Jail February 1907 inWelcome to Leicester, Dahlia Publishing, 2016

His mother was Told to Leave Him Out to Die in Algebra of Owls 2016

How a Dress Lost its Sparkle in The Bosphorus Review (Turkey) 2018

How Do You Rehearse for This? in Poems for Grenfell, Onslaught Press, 2018

How Rapunzel Ends in Prole 2018

I saw Lifejackets Left on the Beach and *The Staircase of Knives* in Well Versed (Morning Star) 2015 and 2018

Icon in Red #C0362C in Amaryllis 2015

I'm Here Wherever that is in Poetica Review 2019

Outside the Photograph and S*tories from 'The Jungle'* in Over Land, Over Sea: poems for those seeking refuge, Five Leaves, 2015

Put a Spell a Those February Blues in The Ofi Press (Mexico) 2018

Reptiles in Texas in Riggwelter 2018

Saving Grace in You Are Not Your Rape, Rhythm 'n' Bones Press, USA, 2018

Standing on Ice in Domestic Cherry 2018

The Landmarks Change When you Walk Home in #MeToo, Fair Acre Press, 2017

The Quilt With 598 Squares in Atrium Poetry 2018

The Significance of a Dress in A Scream of Many Colours, Poetry Space, 2018

When Your Name's Not Smith in And Other Poems 2018

Wishing Not to be Stalled in Poetanoster University of Leicester, 2018

The Significance of A Dress

Contents

I Saw Life Jackets Left on the Beach	8
Stories from *The Jungle*	9
Bridal Dresses in Beirut	13
Dismantling *The Jungle*	14
Outside the Photograph	16
The Significance of a Dress	17
A Boy's Text Message in Headlines	18
I'm Here, Wherever that is	19
Uniforms Contain Humans	20
Diary from Holloway February 1907	22
Reptiles in Texas	24
His Mother was Told to Leave Him Out to Die	25
How do you Rehearse for This?	26
Saving Grace	27
Standing on Ice	28
Staircase of Knives	29
The Quilt With 598 Squares	30
He Did/She Did	32
Today's Lesson Misses the Target	34
This is how Rapunzel Ends	35
Gone Midnight and I Needed to Press Reset	36
Wishing not to be Stalled	37
The Landmarks Change when you Walk Home	38
Icon in Red (#C0362C)	40
Put a Spell on Those February Blues	41
When Your Name's Not Smith	42
The Sea Remembers	43
Where No One Operates the Lights	44
How a Dress Lost its Sparkle	46
An Elephant in Atlantic City	47
The Doctor from Aleppo's Book Keeping	48

I Saw Life Jackets Left on the Beach
Kos, Summer 2015

I asked the waiter, but he shrugged.
Later he loaded crates into the manager's car.
She looked dead on her feet, said something
about an extra sitting at dinner.
But there weren't any new guests.
It was my two weeks in the sun.
I'd eaten nothing but lettuce
for weeks to look OK in my bikini.

The waiter stopped flirting, went quiet.
I followed him to the derelict hotel where tents
had sprung up like mushrooms overnight.
He didn't want to talk. I didn't push it.
You learn that at a call centre. Some people
think you're a machine and they just poke buttons.
Others, you're the only person they've talked to all day.
I'd only come to sunbathe
so helping give out food didn't seem much.

One mother told me men drifted around
and she didn't think her daughters were safe.
After their journey, they didn't want confinement
to a crowded room. I became a chaperone.
I taught them hopscotch on the beach.
Their laughter such a strange sound.
Paperwork's slow at the best of times.
I left my euros for the hotel to pass on.
I hope it helped. I bought them sanitary pads.
People don't think about that:
their bodies capable of creating life.

Stories from *The Jungle*

Everything Abdel sees is smeared, despite his glasses.
With the sleeve of a dusty shirt, he pushes grime
from the middle to the edges of his lenses.
They've witnessed family fall victim to war crimes.
He could shower for a fortnight and never feel clean.
English is an official language in Sudan.
At sixteen he wants to join relatives already in England.

To dodge military conscription, Sayid, 20, fled from Syria.
Inspired by the story of one of his heroes, William Gibson,
Sayid got to Egypt, then packed on a small boat to
Lampedusa,
through Italy to France, from where he can only move on.
On a borrowed laptop he listens to Syrian pop music.
He'd love to cook. He still has to pay a trafficker
weekly for the right to chase lorries to his brother in
England.

With a bandaged hand Abdul, 21, tells of imprisonment
and gestures to describe the electric shocks he received
after his arrest by the Sudanese government.
His tribe also harassed by rebel militia. He feels deceived
by traffickers. Despite his razor-wire injury,
he'll try again. Sudan was an English colony.
He wants to stop looking over his shoulder.

When a tiger stalks, play dead. But it's hard not to run.
When his friends were arrested in Eritrea, Hayat fled
and moved from Ethiopia to Libya and across the
Mediterranean.
He became tiger, his prey an England-bound train. His
hunt failed.
His broken arm cast, he hunkers in a makeshift, tented
cave.
A tiger fails nine of ten hunts. He's five down, four more
to brave.
English is the only European language he speaks.

At Baath University in Homs, His English Literature
studies
were interrupted by conscription. Firas drew and
followed an isopleth.
Three family members were killed by Syrian government
forces,
he couldn't bear to see or be responsible for any more
death.
Skin torn by razor-wire, he still dreams of Oxford spires.
Relatives live in several English towns, all with
universities.
He wants to use the language he's immersed himself in.

Ziad was a respected lawyer in Daara. Now he fidgets, grubby and injured from climbing fences, dodging security and avoiding dogs. The pack of cigarettes crinkles as he weaves it in his fingers, emptying a last curl of tobacco. He didn't smoke them but can't finish with the packet. He translates legal arguments into English. He wants to join relatives and practice law again.

Stories based on newspaper reports. Names have been changed.

Bridal Dresses in Beirut

Each dress hangs from a noose.
One is plain satin with scalloped lace,
another an orgy of tulle,
dreamy organza with applique flowers
hanging from wire
strung between palm trees.
One is short, a shift with a tulip skirt,
the sort of dress picked
in a hurry to satisfy a shotgun
or Article 522.
The breeze breathes through them,
bullies the dresses into ghosts,
brides with no substance,
angels bereft of their voices.

Article 522, since repealed, absolved a rapist who married his victim

Dismantling *The Jungle*
This is a city (French Calais resident visiting the camp for the first time)

He has never been asked his name.
'Bambino,' he says and holds up six fingers.
Someone tells her he's orphaned.

He asks the visitor how she got a cut on her knee.
'No one in Calais ever asked me about that,' she says,
'Calais residents should visit. This is shameful, so shameful.'

A nursery worker, she's drawn to the children.
'I imagined a little camp. This is upsetting.
We have a life, a roof over our heads, a TV.'

The bambinos show her how to play Grandma's
footsteps.
There are libraries, makeshift classrooms, street food,
scents of spices merge with charred canvas and mud.

The visitor asks a thirteen year old about his bandaged head.
He shows her stitches in a wound caused by a rubber bullet,
describes tear gas as 'like onions but worse.'

Radio Jungala blares a babble of voices
simultaneously translated into English.
The children taste new sounds on their tongues.

Soon they will be taken to small centres
in unheated Nissen huts in southern France
where they will no longer recognise the food.

He doesn't know the word for uncle. It will be translated
as cousin. The difference will scupper
his entitlement to settle in England with relatives.

A fire starts. A man adds a discarded desk,
then a chair. Flames lick up the legs,
create a ghostly shape of someone,

an echo of a former life.
The man pulls up sofa, covers it
in tarpaulin and sits to watch.

Another man leaves plant pots near
the mobile registration centre. It's their only
chance to be noticed and tended.

Outside the Photograph

Sea otters don't wear pink, but she looks like one
from a wide angle, drifting with the tide.
The woman's anorak and scarves buoy her.
Zoom in and see her baby, swaddled
in a salmon-coloured sling arranged
so she lies on her mother's heartbeat, exhausted.
Her mother looks beyond the borders
of the photograph, towards the coastguard's boat.
These two will be rescued.
Clammy as wet clothes, memories will cling.
The mother's journey will pass into family lore.
The girl will later be puzzled as to why
she can only get to sleep
when she's lulled by lapping water
and the feel of another's heart.

The Significance of a Dress
Refugee camp northern Iraq

Even if home is makeshift and her carriage is a borrowed
pair of shoes that dance over gravel baked in the desert
heat,
a bride still wants to feel special, at least for one day.
No one can afford to buy when twenty neighbours share
a latrine and there's a constant vigil against disease.
Tulin, named after a daughter, offers gown hire, make-up
and hairstyling that will withstand humid evenings.
'I don't ask how old they are,' says the beautician. A
mural
outside shows a girl in a white gown holding a teddy
bear.
The future is tomorrow. Next year is a question.
A wedding is a party, a welcome, a sign of hope.
The dresses sparkle with sun-reflected diamante
but the gravel paths of the camp leave the hems stained.

A Boy's Text Message in Headlines

Fifteen people rescued by one boy's text
Pashto-speaking boy, fleeing Taliban, sends text
Unaccompanied minor texts for help
Boy texts in broken English.

Fifteen refugees saved from suffocation
Fifteen migrants found close to death
Fifteen immigrants found in lorry container
Fifteen immigrants, assumed illegal, detained

One man arrested for illegally assisting entry to UK
Arrest made as police investigate lorry containing
migrants
Police investigate immigrants in lorry, arrest made
Frumpy: Duchess of Cambridge in Indian-designer dress

The text read: *I ned halp darivar no stap car no oksijan in the car no sagnal iam in the cantenar. Iam no jokan valla.* [*valla* – I swear to God]

I'm Here, Wherever that is

It took two years to get here.
I couldn't find it on a map.
It's not London. It's damp.
I was given thirty-five pounds,
and have to skip meals
when I pay for English lessons.

I'd sit and stare at walls
until I found the library.
There's no time limit.
I hear foreign tongues
in the next room: neither
English nor my language.

I said 'Hi' to someone
without averting my eyes today.
She said 'How are you?'
I know to say 'Fine,' now.
The grey lifted, momentarily.
I saw a map. I still don't know
where here is, but I now know
it's two letters from home.

Uniforms Contain People

I
My uniform
is decorated: a Bronze Star and Purple Heart.
My uniform
took me to Bosnia, Iraq, Afghanistan.
My uniform
brought me back home.

My uniform
covered wounds.
My uniform
covered my body.
My uniform
identified me.

My uniform
is so interwoven with the fabric of me
I can't just take it off.

II
A man who has not served
eyes an easy distraction.
He pictures a wave of support
from those still waiting
for the Steel Industry Revival
while Rust Belt Democrats squirm.
He pictures a military cowed
by the magnificence of office.
One tweet and no one's
talking about his son-in-law.

III
People saw
my uniform.

People saw
what I did.
People assessed
my skills, my ability, my fitness.

People did not
see my gender.
People did not
care about the cost of my transition.

People care
when the military is under-resourced.
People know
the army is more than its hardware.

People saw
my uniform.

Diary from Holloway Jail February 1907

Alice Hawkins 1863-1946; suffragette, wife to Alfred, mother to six

I

6am the prison is holding its breath:
those moments before the electric lights click on.
Muscle-memory folds the two rough blankets
over the flat pillows and counterpane
while we clean and stretch out the night's cramps.
Breakfast is invariably a pint of tea and brown loaf.

Why is an equally-experienced and educated widow
and parent paid less than a childless man?
I couldn't find an answer in the Trade Unions
who didn't think of women as breadwinners.
I worked and worked but if anything happened
to Alfred, my work was worthless.

II

8am Chapel 10am Exercise Even damp
air is welcomed. Talk is banned so one
can only watch and guess another's crime.

Some have babies. Imagine being born
in a cage. Will they learn to sing?

III
11am back in cells until dinner:
haricot beans and potatoes
or pressed meat and potatoes
or suet pudding and potatoes
all with brown bread.

Refused entry when Winston Churchill
spoke at Leicester's Palace Theatre.
Alfred had to speak for me.
Without my vote, how can a politician
stand on a democratic platform?

IV
4pm Tea is a pint of cocoa
and loaf of brown bread.

I was told, 'Get back to your family.'
One son joined the Army, another the Navy.
Both could vote, but me, the woman
who brought them into the world,
how could I have no say?

V
8pm Lights off I stretch on a mattress
where you feel everything and ache.
Room just a degree too cold to soften
the course weaves and welcome sleep.
Fresh bruises to count in the morning.

Reptiles in Texas

The First Lady faces the edge
of a flood as if it will give way for her.
In Anahuac, 350 alligators watch their pens fill
while employees sit on boats, guns ready.
They've all day and no homes to return to.
In Cosby, the Arkema plant could explode.
A fanged eel washes up in Texas City.
An aid convoy snakes up from Mexico.
Wall or no wall, Mexicans help Texas work.
The President declares a National Day
of Prayer and offers a million dollars,
that won't undo building on flood plains,
or the intensity of Harvey.

His Mother was Told to Leave Him Out to Die

His hand bones were wrapped in linen bags
made by children from King Richard III school
and laid in a lead coffin surrounded by oak.
A layer of concrete to support
the Kilkenny marble plinth and tombstone
of Swaledale fossil stone
dotted with coal, a dash of amber
and two unfossilised shark's teeth.
The three hundred and fifty piece
pietra dura shield included
lapis lazuli from Afghanistan,
Tuscan yellow and white chalcedony,
brown English Ashburton marble
and Duke's Red stone specifically ordered
from a limited source at Chatsworth.
Six lions each with a nineteen piece
mosiac for their heads.
Sunlight on the minimal cross
leaves the shadow of a sword.

How Do you Rehearse for This?

Someone switches the warehouse radio off,
a signal for another one minute vigil
and the noisy office falls silent like an audience
sensing a show's about to begin.
The ash and black tower block skeleton
could belong to a flickering war movie.
Critics shout who the murderer is before
a blaze of detectives secure the scene,
even before the victims are known.
In the interval, the audience donate
to crowdfunders and open homes.
The director hides in the bar, the prompter
loses the script, the technician can't manoeuvre
the spotlight. There's a call for the scriptwriter,
who's suffering from concussion after walking
into a lighting rig the floor manager failed
to move, and clings desperately to anything
but the truth. The lights splutter out.
The stage turns cold and looks even darker.
The players are abandoned.
Survivors blink at their new-found fame
but fifteen minutes now is worse than the prior
waiting in the wings, shushed into accepting
cut corners, poor wiring and cheap costumery.
The audience take their selfies and move on.
The players sense they are supposed to shuffle
off stage. They put one foot forward, testing
their weight on the boards, fingers outstretched
to feel for obstacles as they inch towards shadows.

Saving Grace

After Easter she changed. The powder-blue ribbon
on her ponytail had been swapped for a red one. She'd
no longer slip her hand in mine and wait to be spoken to.

She hung back at playtime, waiting to see if the janitor
was around. She'd talk to him as she'd always done,
but now she'd stroke his arm and smile as she spoke.

If not the janitor, the male teacher. But he'd step away,
return her to friends and hopscotch. When her friend's
father sat on a bench, she eased herself next to him,

unable to reach his arms, she stroked his thigh
and tried to swing her legs over so she could sit in
his lap. He stood up. She looked as if she'd been hit.

I asked about the new ribbon. Red was her uncle's
favourite colour. He liked it when she wore it.
He liked her to touch his arms, smile and sit on his lap.

I asked if she liked it. She asked if she was in trouble.
A summer birthday, she was the youngest in the class.
Her uncle was planning a special party, a secret.

Seven isn't a special age. For once, social services
worked. She asked if it was OK not to be sad she wasn't
going to see him again. The blue ribbon was back.

Standing on Ice

(Athabasca Glacier)

After the novelty of standing on ice
in walking boots, not blades,
I watch my daughter grin: she'll boast
about being on a glacier back at school.
She's already taller than me.
Cradled by a mountain range,
this glacier is slowly receding,
gradually changing the landscape.
Tourists, shivering and wary
of sliding, return to the bus.
We linger in the knowledge
the glacier will outlive us.
For now, we can absorb
the moment while the glacier melts
and my daughter grows
and I stand in the calm of ice-borne air.

The Staircase of Knives

The only thing that's regular
is that there are two on each stair,
one at either end. She has to thread
her way past these kitchen knives
stabbed into the white-painted treads
to get to bed. She has to tip-toe:
if disturbed they will invade
her dreams and sharpen her nerves.

They are not the most chilling
thing in the photo posted by police.
That honour goes to the bullet.
Against the stark white,
its tip points to a blank wall.
This is someone's home,
'a place where one lives,
especially as part of a family.'

The Quilt with 598 Squares

Mayurathy Perinpamoorihy, Amandeep Kaur Hothi,
Helen Skudder, Anita Harris,
Agnieszka Dziegielewska, Sandra Boakes, Penny Ann
Taylor, Raheela Imran,

Sylvia Rowley-Bailey is stitched in pink beads
on Laura Ashley-style fabric. She was sitting
at her computer when found with twenty-three
knife wounds, deemed only worth five years
because she 'nagged' her partner and murderer.

Laura Wilson, Kerry Smith, Claire Parrish, Hollie
Gazzard, Gail Lucas,
Camille Mathurasingh, Natasha Trevis, Carol French,
Rachael Slack, Victoria Rose

A gold crescent moon and stars adorn a navy patch
for a teacher and author, Julie Ann Semper.
Her boyfriend was 'too anxious' to attend court.
The judge warned he'd enter
a guilty plea and try him in his absence.

Kayleigh Palmer, Yvonne Davies, Mariam Mohdaqi, Kate
McHugh, Karren Martin,
Paula Newman, Annie Beaver, Desirie Thomas, Eystna
Blunnie, Sally Harrison

'This was an isolated incident,' say the police.
Neighbours and colleagues say
he 'was hard-working, loving dedicated'
and he 'should not be remembered
for his actions on that day.'

Nazia Aktar, Taylor Burrows, Sally Cox...
What were their stories?
Cerys Yemm, Farkhanda Younis, Svetlana Zolotovska.
Who speaks for those whose voices were murdered?

He Did/She Did

He tosses branded products, conveniently at eye level,
into the shopping cart. She slips them back on the shelves
and bends or stretches to pick replacement unbranded goods.

His work wardrobe is three suits and six shirts.
Hers is crammed to bursting with cheap separates
that she can mix up to look like new outfits.

He suggests splitting the bills so he pays half
and she pays half. He earns twice what she makes,
so a greater proportion of her earnings go on bills.

His cellphone calendar is business meetings and Dodgers'
games. Hers is birthdays, relatives' health appointments,
children's playdates, shopping reminders and chores.

He slips his keys in his pocket to run to the store for milk.
She holds her keys in her hand, keeps her eyes down
but still hears wolf-whistles and gets told to smile.

His working day is uninterrupted and runs smoothly.
She runs errands in her break, takes calls from their son,
his school and cheers that soccer practice is cancelled.

They report being robbed. His statement is taken without question.
She's still trying to figure out the relevance of her skirt length
and heel height and why she gets asked what she was doing there.

He shrugs and asks what the fuss is about.
She puts on her pink hat, picks up her pink placard
and tells him she doesn't know when she'll be home.

Today's Lesson Misses the Target

Children shouldn't see a stranger
come into their classroom,
pull out a gun
and aim at the teacher.
According to tweets, the gunman,
an estranged husband,
should have waited for his wife
to come home,
because a husband killing his wife
should only be done at home,
where children are witnesses;
because children shouldn't see a stranger
come into their classroom,
pull out a gun,
and aim at their teacher.

How Rapunzel Ends

He calls his girlfriend Rapunzel,
after the girl in the tower with nothing
to do except clean and sing.
She falls in love with the first
person she sees who doesn't look
like her imprisoner. He says she broke
his heart and he wants her back.

He sets up a piano on a patch
of green outside the council offices
near one of the city's busiest
streets. He puts up boards urging
passersby to like and support him
on social media. An action that asks
people to take sides, preferrably his.

She's immune to emotional blackmail.
This isn't a fairytale. He wasn't her prince.

Gone Midnight and I Needed to Press Reset

Eardrums still reverberating, my mood was all wrong.
One moment was high alert, the next anger and disbelief.
What could be calmer than a graveyard? Natural shadows
from trees were a balm to a country girl who'd felt welcome
until tonight. I was used to being told it wasn't a girl's job,
heard the same banter many times over, but never been touched,
groped or assaulted until now. It's just a moment's lapse.
Instead of being first to leave, I'd mis-judged by seconds
and bunched with a crowd. Fool me once... I'd not leave my job.
I would still do what I loved. But I needed to hit stop
and refuse to rewind. Refuse the post-mortem of blame.
This wasn't my fault. The rustle of leaves reassured me.
The graves remind me history doesn't stop even if life does.
The notice board's Cyrillic script looks like the scrawled notes
I'd made to write my review from. A deadline looms.
But for now I have St George's Churchyard, its ambience
whispers that I can slay that dragon, I will survive tomorrow.

Wishing Not to be Stalled

I am glad it is going slowly - you don't deserve a bullet Uma Thurman

A relief from the worry of a crowded space
and groping hands. Here I can ride solo.
A space from tossing a coin as to whether
to walk home or, post-Worboys, get a taxi.
An open box that allows witnesses.
Its movement a reminder you're part of a chain
connected to compartments above and below,
as they are: it's not just you. A hashtag can be
brushed off, mansplained, but each dismissal
strengthens the links. I might be alone in this
paternoster but it's not the same aloneness
as when I was threatened, dodged fumbles,
told, whilst wearing school uniform, I could earn
extra in my lunch break in the red light district;
when I was the only woman in a venue watching
a band I had to review. #MeToo. I stand
in this compartment, dare myself to go over the top
and pray the momentum continues the revolution.

The Landmarks Change When You Walk Home

Tuck your hair and scarf under your jacket and zip it
so it can't get grabbed. Why did you bring a bag?
Don't you have pockets? Hold your keys in your hand.
Can you run in those heels? Should've worn jeans.
Play a brisk walking rhythm in your head, something edgy
and noisy and hope the mood is reflected in your expression.
There's the 'Cheer Up Love, It Might Never Happen' Spot.
Here's the 'It's Your Lucky Night' Clock Tower –
an offer I didn't take up. Here's the 'Avoid At All Costs'
Underpass, even if you have to wait for the light to go red.
Here's the Please Keep Your Eyes On The Road
Railway Bridge. It ends at Wolf-whistle Stretch, but keep
your speed constant. You can't rest if you get out
of breath. Don't wait if a car approaches the junction
you have to cross, walk further along, cross further
down and walk back. Repeat as often as necessary.
I know it adds to the journey but think of the extra
calories burned. Here's Polo Road where four buddies
wanted the birthday boy to lose his virginity. I figured
I could make the dead end before them and hoped
they wouldn't get out and run after me. Here's Number
Eleven – the age of the boy who asked for sex, who was bigger
and heavier despite his age. Go past Proposition Lamppost.
I don't think I need to explain, do I? Don't look. Keep up.

That day I stupidly wore those clacky heels, this is Talk
To Yourself Loudly Street, where I hoped the two men
who'd already seen me wouldn't be interested in a mad woman.
This is News Corner where nipping out for a Sunday paper
in paint-splattered clothes won me a suitor with a wedding
ring willing to pay. I said no, obvs. Skip That Street: among
the run down, MOT-failures, a silver Mercedes was found,
owner in the boot, her throat garroted. She had a wedding ring
too. You're slowing, keep up, not far now. Unless that family
saloon circles again. I was about to Turn To My Front Door
when the driver asked how much. I told him he only
drove a Ford and he sped off. But I still had to walk round
the block to make sure he didn't know I lived here
on my ordinary street at the end of my ordinary walk home.

Icon in Red (#C0362C)

It started as a span of red cross-stitches,
more for the uprights; suspension wires
in backstitch: an icon on an embroidered map.
It drew the eye and came to dominate the view.

It provided a backdrop for internet searches,
lists of places to see, checking local weather,
lists of things to pack, the endless checking,
parsing unsolicited advice for useful tips.

It became real. The absence of the famous fog
offered panoramic views and I admired,
not the feat of engineering, but the desire
to link communities in careful red stitches.

International Orange CMYK 0,72,77,24; RGB 192,54,44, hex #C0362C
embroidery thread DMC 3777

Put a Spell on Those February Blues

Ella Fitzgerald, De Montfort Hall Leicester 28/2/62

The lights dim. People tap feet on the maple sprung
floor.
If it weren't for the chairs, they'd shuffle along
to a half-known rhythm. Cigarette fog provides cover
as the orchestra take their places. Players run
through their last minute rituals. The audience still.
No backing dancers, no gimmicks, no dazzling visuals.
Complete confidence in musicians building into the
thrill,
putting voice centre stage. A voice with no rival.
A quintet, songs, a microphone and Ella.

When Your Name's Not Smith

While he writes I imagine taking his form
and folding it into a paper boat, perhaps filling
his letter tray with water from the cooler
to see if the boat floats or sinks, if ink will

seep from paper to water and colour it.
Family legend has it that some great, great
relative decided to run to the sea, away
from weaving or sheep farming. His name

was a barrier so he changed it to fit in.
He didn't think some distant niece would end
up standing in a bank watching a teller fill
out a form with a name I said I'd spell, but

he asserted he knew how to spell it.
His biro skims the page while I jam my hands
into my pockets in case they follow
my desire to snatch the artificial daisy

from its plastic vase, tear off each petal,
he knows my name, he knows it not.
He asks me to sign his form. I tell him
I can't: my name is not spelt correctly.

The Sea Remembers

The night waves lap with a journey's rhythm:
one step after another after another.

I imagine Europe in colour and daytime
with buildings that are still intact
despite beaches littered with lifejackets.

The waves are ceaseless and push
layers of shingle in a wash of salt water.

Clouds swell, heavy with storm.
The rubber boat rises and falls
as the sea flares and recedes.

The waves' rhythm reminds me of a song,
a romantic tune my father used to hum.

He said he was old, heavy as a sack
of rubble and anchored in our home
where the only walls are memories.

The waves call me back to this tattoo
that may yet soften into melody.

Where No one Operates the Lights

The lights never go off.
To sleep you burrow
under your foil blanket
and curl up like a cub.

Instead of sheep, count
children, twenty per cage.

Don't multiply to account
for how many cages.

If you need more numbers,
count the water bottles,
packs of chips, how many
children can sleep on one mat.

I don't know who she is but I
change her diaper. There aren't any toys

so she's my doll. Don't think
about why there's no dust on the wire.

The guard's gun is like the one
put to my brother's head.
To go back is death.
To stay here is purgatory.

Last night I dreamt of a lamp
beside a golden door

as I lie burrowed in a place
where the lights never go off.

How a Dress Lost its Sparkle

'Why did they discard their clothes on the beach?'
he repeats, as if another asking will adjust the answer
to one he wants to hear. He thinks mothers should launder

their own children's clothes. He's not placated by the answer
that discarded clothes are washed, dried and recycled
for the next boatload, for the next and the next.

Above him is Arabella Dorman's *Suspended*,
discarded clothing gathered from beaches held
by wires and illuminated by a spherical lamp

that alternates between yellow and bright
white light, sun and moon. The clothes are flat,
no longer needing three dimensions to cover bodies.

Amongst them is a long-sleeved, ankle length pink dress
to fit a five-year-old, covered in a layer of gold gauze.
A special occasion dress that sparkles as the light changes.

A dress that doesn't warm on cold nights, that shows dirt
and sweat, that absorbs salt water and fears, that, if pulled
over a mouth, would hide the bit lip that stops tears.

It won't launder without soap and what does its wearer wear
while it's washed? A closer look reveals a tide mark of salt,
an obstinate, rusty stain. Mementos no one wants to keep.

Suspended by Arabella Dorman is an art installation hosted by Leicester
Cathedral during the Journeys Festival.

An Elephant in Atlantic City

Atlantic City's elephant stands on a pedestal,
trunk up like a salesman drumming up trade.
The seats strapped to the back of this bull
are empty, the blanket on his back gilded
with pyrite. The casino advertised, the Taj Mahal,
is shut. The elephant is white. His sculptor unpaid.
At his feet a banner declaring 'Trump', left whole
and undamaged. Knock and it sounds hollow.

The Doctor from Aleppo's Book Keeping

Injuries need fixing

They are not anti- or pro-
regime.

One side blacklisted me.

No matter whom they belong to.

People feel protective of their tribe.

it was dangerous to support
the other side.

I had to flee.

The boat sank.

Eleven hours my one focus

to keep my head above water.

I had to try again.

I built a network of
connections.

Fifteen contacts find clients.

I could buy boats.

I bribe the Turkish police.

Turkey to Italy or Greece

Onward travel to Germany

onward travel to
Scandinavia

Destination isn't my
concern.

Bribes, boats, costs mount up.

The UN could do this.

If I stay in Syria, I'll be killed.

I send my son to safety.

My family needed safety.

Water feels safer than land right now.

Not drowning is an art, a drive

I was rescued to try again.

I failed and failed again.

People trust doctors.

I pay gangs to run the boats.

I've sent eight thousand people

No sinking or drownings so far.

costs four thousand five hundred euros.

plus two thousand euros or

plus four thousand euros.

I didn't want to charge.

I need to feed my own family.

Let people travel legally.

If I travel,

I've a 50% chance of survival.

I dream of making a home again.